Rupture

Rupture

Clementine Morrigan

DEMETER

DEMETER PRESS, BRADFORD, ONTARIO

Published by:
Demeter Press
140 Holland Street West
P. O. Box 13022
Bradford, ON L3Z 2Y5
Tel: (905) 775-9089
Email: info@demeterpress.org
Website: www.demeterpress.org

Demeter Press logo based on Skulptur "Demeter"
by Maria-Luise Bodirsky <www.keramik-atelier.bodirsky.edu>

Library and Archives Canada Cataloguing in Publication

Morrigan, Clementine, 1986–
Rupture / Clementine Morrigan.

ISBN 978-1-927335-08-6

1. Morrigan, Clementine, 1986–. 2. Sexual abuse victims—Rehabilitation. 3. Sexual abuse victims—Canada—Biography. I. Title.

RC560.S44M67 2012 362.82'924092 C2012-907264-8

Printed and Bound in Canada

to the silenced — may you find your voice

contents

part one: wordless

part two: kicked dog

part six: better for it

part one: wordless

moonless

when he touches me it's like electricity
because i've never seen the moon
i'm all lit up like a christmas tree
because i've never seen the moon
and his fingertips trace pathways of ecstasy
i am blinded by the bright white lines
like roads and rivers on a map that glows
and glows and leads me nowhere
i am divided as he divides me
my eyes are closed
i have not said yes and i have not said no
but it feels good, so
i have never seen the moon
wild eyes at midnight, spinning in my room
the ceilings hide the skies
and i think i've never been so high
but i know nothing of heights
because i have never seen the sky
i am sparkling to pieces
disembodied, bodied
i am loving the way he is touching me
i've never felt anything better
but i've never felt anything much
i am living in a blinding darkness
and i have never seen the moon

wordless

the feelings, they don't take the shape
of words
anymore
it is guttural, a pounding
a shaking and a writhing on the floor
a calling out to the Goddesses
that i can't do this anymore
i have been here before
when the fullness fills up too much
and it has nowhere to go but out

when what happened is too much
when it was happening you split it
into pieces
remembered only what you needed to
to make it through that moment
but now that it is over
the pieces that you separated
slide
and crash into one another
causing explosions
you can't handle
causing pictures which disturb
and you shudder

this can only be expressed in a language
that has no words, a language

of sounds like an animal
and movements, the unfreezing
of the frozen body
the contortion of limbs and facial muscles
an expression of anguish
left wordless because there never were
the words

whole

i am the one who is neither
one nor two
who belongs in many places
and belongs nowhere at all
i am the one who is many
who has been many more
i am stunted by the severing
i prefer to be whole

zombie apocalypse

it's going to hurt this much
and then you aren't going to feel anything
for a long, long time
so cling to your lover like they or you is dying
and imagine a zombie apocalypse and realize
you don't even know who you'd want
to be running with
and then lie on the floor and imagine
it's the ceiling and then realize
you don't even feel like crying
you aren't even sure if you feel anything
or if you ever did
and then think about cornfields
and barns you used to sneak into alone
or drunk with your sister
and remember when you were so filled up
with burning hope and you were so willing
to destroy everything because you believed
somehow that there must be more
there had to be

addict

i can swallow the whole sky
so no bottle can fill me
no bottle will ever be enough
i am awakened once again
by an urgency
fulfillment of a prophecy
what i'll have will have me
hold me
and in the morning
sick with fragmented memory
i will swear that i am done
never again will i chase the void
that endless hollow
but my thirst is endless too
and i have already begun

i follow sidewalks
which glitter and shine
with shattered glass
and i will add to the mess
i follow alleyways which lead me
nowhere except for
back to this

femme

severed and stitched back together
a language that was never mine
i use the language of femininity
cut up and rearranged
redefine
resignify
i use the same symbols
but i make them mean
something else
are you baffled by my appropriation
of prettiness?
i smell like a dude and i dress like a slut
and i am continuously punished for being
too much
i am made an example of

(my femininity is not an invitation
i am not here for you
your gaze does not bring me into
existence
i exist without you
and i do not desire you
i did not put on this outfit to impress you
and i don't care what you think of
my armpit hair or my
guitar skills
leave me the fuck alone)

oh the sex

my foot in your hand is beautiful
like a shell
and you hold it with more love
than you could hold a child

like dying

there is no end to the endlessness
we steal the night
still the night
distill the night
we drank the night
it was gold hot in our blood like dying
and we did die
over and over again
we were wedded to nothing
we couldn't feel the pain
it was cold and we pissed in bushes
and we didn't fucking care

how many times
have i scraped my body
off the sidewalk?
how many times
have i picked up
the broken smashed bits of me?

filling up on fantasy

no, i don't want to explain my poetry
i can't tell you what it means, what it meant
the way i coaxed meaning
from hollow moments
the way i longed and longed for nothing
nothing in particular
the way i sat in the grass
in the pouring rain
and laughed and laughed
and thought it was love
sure it was
it had to be
because it felt like lightning
and glitter and pure electricity
it felt like being lifted up out of my skin
abandoning my body
being reignited, reunited
with my poetry
restored to meaning
and it was this boy and that boy
and the other who was there
manifested as human, incarnate
everything i wanted
and needed them to be

silence

my rib cage is like the branches of a tree only
slightly more regular
i wish you could touch the textures of my bones
i pluralize out of politeness because i assume
there must be more
i'm expecting to be taken there
the veins on a leaf are like the veins in my arm
they change colour in the sun
am i speaking?
because i cannot hear the words

sobriety

the stillness of staying with myself
the ache of days and days and nights
the inability to feel this but i do
i could run, to the bottle
to the blade, to the endless distractions
the flashing lights that have guided me
nowhere for years
but i stay
i stay

gratitude

i am so grateful for all these plants
each with their own shape and scent
thickness of leaf, personality
i am so grateful for the tall, wise trees
silent or singing softly in the breeze:
they have always been here for me
comforted me, called to me
and welcomed my embrace
i am so grateful for the rain
outside my window now
gaining momentum
washing and quenching it all

the way back

the way back is like a path in a dark forest
it's diving into deep cold water with
my eyes wide open
it's like pebbles and stones under my bare feet

the way back is like the sky at night without a breeze
a stillness so infinite it is eerie
the way back is the freezing cold of winter
and the clarity of a bright gray sky
the way back is looking at myself in the mirror
and seeing who is really there
the soul behind those eyes

the roar inside the bottle
is like the sound inside the seashell
you think it's the whole ocean but it's not
it's just a single shell
and you could stand there your whole life
listening to it
and never find your way back
to the sea

i want the sea, i want my heart
i want my words back

divine responsibility

self love is a divine responsibility
because the goddess Herself makes
no mistakes
i am as sacred as each tree
each squirrel running past me
as sacred as the sky in all her
expansiveness and each shade she
possesses, i am as sacred
as the morning, the cool air in the
autumn, i am as sacred as the bees
it is my responsibility to love and to
heal myself, to free myself
to do the work that is
recovery: the regaining of something
lost or taken away
the restoration of my relationship
with myself, the restoration of my
wholeness: integrity
to do this work is not selfish or
self indulgence, it is a manifestation
of the goddess and her divine
intention for me
it is my responsibility

part two: kicked dog

rot

my heart clenches when i see your picture. i could never write you the love poems i wanted you to have. you were my baby, precious, i wanted to take care of you. but you know loving me is like loving a blade: i'm pretty, shiny but hard to hold. i was more than your whore but i was that too. spread eagle on your bed or my legs up over my head, it was always up to you. you'd shiver, quiver shake. fucking a goddess, the earth cracks, opens. the snow falls, clings to the leaves on the trees, killing them. you wrap your fingers around my skeleton, trying to make love to it, but the love's been gone a long time and i can't stand it but i do. i let you in reluctantly. i open my gates so you won't have to smash them open, because you would never, right? the violence was so subtle but my seams are split, i've been fucked sick. i go into the bathroom, suck on my fingers, shiver through the fever of another winter. i want to ask you what you remember. do you remember the sound of falling feathers? your sweet baby is crying. did you fuck her too much, too hard, too long? or maybe she just doesn't love you anymore.

kicked dog

we pushed it because we couldn't believe. we didn't know what you'd do to me. we wanted to see how hard we had to push it before it would break. we laughed about it. we were terrified. and then i'm on the floor with you on top of me screaming in my face and no i don't want to die. you can push a body to see if it will break. so forceful the drywall behind me is crushed like a leaf. it was your hands that did this to me. you loved me. now you are in jail for what you did to me. we laughed about it. we couldn't believe it. we were like children and we were taking it too far. you hurt me. grabbed my wrists pressed bruises into them. put your knee on my chest, pressed my solar plexus with all your weight, breaking blood vessels and taking my breath from me. wouldn't it be strange if you killed me? my body still alive. crumpled on the floor. crying and sobbing like a little girl. apologizing. i'm not sure. i'm just sorry. i love you so much. i shouldn't have said what i said or did what i did, whatever i did, i shouldn't have done it. i tried so hard to avoid it but waiting for your rage was terrifying. like a dog, i was shaking. i was always waiting. i was always wondering when you were going to start again. i don't remember. you didn't remember. we learned to erase what happened so that we could forgive each other and do it again. then i would see it coming. you start picking fights over nothing. i want it to be over so i make it begin. i act like a bitch. you treat me like one. you kick me like a dog. i am one.

making meaning out of the meaningless

because, i told you i can't stand myself, don't want to be around myself and when i go into the forest alone at night there is the fear that i will be raped or killed. and because when i go alone in the day time there is the walk there and back, and sometimes i sing songs and the people watch me from their cars and it is better that way. but i am still alone. and sometimes the trees do talk to me but then i have to wonder if it's real or if it means anything without some random boy or man to watch me and to think i'm eccentric and strange and to sigh and think to himself "that strange girl is mine." but the truth is, he doesn't think those things. he doesn't notice my romance with the trees or my eyes straining for fairies while all the while wondering if he sees me looking, looking for them and looking for him looking for me looking for them. no. he sees the sky as a great big invitation and we lie on the train tracks together and we sit in the middle of an eight lane highway and we are reckless with our lives and we are alive.

he sees the trees and he wants to climb them. i am too afraid. i'm afraid that i'll hurt myself, twist my ankle and i won't be able to walk home. and it's true, i probably will. i am also too afraid to jump off the swings and i have always wanted to. but when i am with him i feel so alive. my pantyhose are ripped almost clear in half and my lips are stained red from dehydration and alcoholism and it makes me feel proud. and i think everyone is staring at us because we are beautiful and rebellious because our lives have some kind of meaning in the pointless spontaneity we create for ourselves. but really no one is looking. no one cares.

i would be the boy

and i am writing this because i don't exist, because i didn't exist and i didn't love him. we laid in his sleeping bag in nathan phillips square and i was hallucinating without any drugs and i could feel the connectivity of the universe and i remember putting on my shoes and leaving him there. because i didn't fucking care. i would be the boy who would watch myself kiss the trees and i would think "isn't she strange? that strange girl is mine." i would be the boy who says "we gotta start a fire" and i would start one like it was nothing without a care in the world or a thought of forest fires. i would be the boy who suggested we needlessly risk our lives by walking the length of the train bridge, way up in the air. i would be the boy climbing trees and sleeping on the sidewalk and throwing fire and fucking this girl or that girl. and falling in love and wearing my grey toque and getting a little apartment with a gas burner stove and lighting up the joints the way they do in jail. and i wouldn't be worried constantly that my body is a fuckable thing, even if i am being objectified, because somehow i am unaware of that objectification or at least indifferent to it. somehow i am moving through the moments from one to the next and this is how i feel.

but it doesn't mean i don't wake up in agony. and it doesn't mean i don't fuck that girl harder each time, trying to feel something, because really, i don't feel anything anymore either.

but i'm not him. these aren't the things that i think and these aren't the things that i do. i watched him do them. i wore the twenty dollar necklace that he gave me and i loved it. it was the nicest thing that i was ever given and it reminded me forever of that summer, that summer of him. and i threw it out willingly, gave it away to the dumpster gods, to prove my love to the one i think i really did love who hurt me so bad, broke the places inside that i didn't even know weren't broken before. broke them so bad that i didn't even care about the magic anymore, i just wanted it to hold still so that i could believe for one second longer.

surfacing

it's okay to go down to the bottom of the ocean. and it's okay to come up for air. you don't have to stay there. it's okay that it pulled you, you couldn't resist the tide. it's okay that it called you. the beautiful song inside a seashell. it's okay that you went, that you followed your feet down there. that you heard the horizon sweetly kissing the sea. and you wanted to touch it, to taste it, to submerge. it's okay that you wanted it and when the waves closed above your head you felt no fear. it was descent, heaven sent, and yes, you were descending. that beautiful foreclosure as the surface of the lake stilled, your body disappeared beneath it. it's okay that you sunk. that the water filled your lungs. the drowning was the best. you suffocated, choked. you let your body be a stone and found you didn't die. you could see for miles and miles in that dark blue sea. that endlessness. and you stayed for years, submerged in that wetness. it's okay that you went. and it's okay to come back to the surface.

the light divided

surfaces, hard and soft. soft bones. sweet. i will use the same words. stars. to form the whole. fractured. the ceilings, the ceilings and the stars. the lines of light we stared at and counted. the light divided. the cold cold space between stars. emptiness and timelessness and raspberry juice still staining my fingertips from times that mattered so much more than this. sweetness. diluted. i make a promise to keep it. to insist on meaning, i mean this. believe it. he isn't sure if i'm deceiving. because my eyes are so full but simultaneously empty and he wants to understand. sometimes i feel like the sky unconquered. because they've got my body now, labeled it out and named it like maps of this earth, owned it, divided it, bulldozed and cemented it but they still have to stare up at those endless, endless stars. he looks into my eyes and they are the untamed heavens. the indiscernible meaning of my smile. am i mocking him? would i dare? and half the time i'm just flirting but my intelligence ups the stakes, makes it cut like a knife, this isn't a game anymore. oh baby, i am sweet like a placid sky. don't worry, nightfall is still a ways off and you can't see my diamonds yet, shining, shining, making you feel so insecure. it's still evening. there's still time. and when my eyes begin to shine you can run and hide. or you can get on top of me, to crush and conquer me. that's not fair, you'll say, that's not fair. but i still long for entanglement and i search the endless surfaces for textures that suggest an emptiness that leads to an endlessness as great as my own.

my madness is resistance

my madness is not an illness. push, push, push, i only snap under the pressure of trying to be something other than who i am. who i am is full and overflowing, the overflow can take many forms like sentences that drip and drip and run on and ideas that push their way out of my lips and the insane idea that my body is my own, my own resistance is often rendered a symptom by those who would have me docile and contained, the tears that well up in my eyes at the intensity of emotion, words that rip right through me and a recognition of synchronicity and the humanity of all. the life of all. i remember being in the psych ward and they were telling me about religious freedom, that we were free to practice our faith as we saw fit. i remember wondering what they would say if i said i was a witch. them, who wouldn't even let me have two interpretations of the same event. my craziness: the bottle glass slicing me up and the breath that returned at the sight of the red, but this must be crazy. i was just making sure i'm still alive. i was just reaffirming that this body is mine, has been mine all this time. windowlessness and mirrorlessness, they gave me no surfaces to see myself with, no glass to reflect or to see through, watch my reflection superimposed on the trees. it was dull orangegray of muted streetlamps pulsing and buzzing with a soundless suffocation, muted again by whatever whiteness they used to hide the view. and i laid on the rubber mattress stripped of my glasses and my dignity, my personhood and my right to see. crazy. crazy? well, so they say. they blame it on my brain, the chemicals are imbalanced and communicating incorrectly and even then, at fifteen, i knew they were full of shit. so i mirrored back to them their bullshit, swallowed their pills and got the fuck out of there. my madness is not an illness, it's a resistance to the pushing and the squeezing that tries to turn me into something other than who i am. who i am is a living being, divine, and within each cell i contain the universe and all of the universe contains all of me. and if it's too much, well, by whose standards? too much, that i should overflow and multiply, that i should feel 1000 shades of every colour, that i should long for the validation of my pain, that i should insist that i deserve more and deserve better than this. it is resistance that they wish to shut out, like they shut out the night, like they dim and dull the stars.

ghosts

ghosts line up with the insides of my bones, the lining of my skull, they fill that space between bone and brain, cushioning the soft tissue, blanketing away the pain. ghosts do eat, they do sleep, they do dream but they don't have to. they have conversations on the insides of my bones, they thicken my blood with their decisions. ghosts are funny, the way they appear, disappear, reappear. the way they keep tricks up their sleeves, to make you think they're going to leave but they don't. when you talk in your sleep it's the ghosts getting out. when you scream in your sleep and i hold you close to me, trying to wake you, shake the ghosts from you and they mingle with mine. your ghosts are beautiful, regretful, delightful. your ghosts have sun in their skin. i think i can hear the ocean. your ghosts are warm like living things. my ghosts are transparent, translucent and cold. they do not grow old. they never died, they were always this way. cushioning my brain until the doctors punctured my spine and freed them into the entirety of my insides, between bones. they leak into my organs, aligning themselves with ever fluid, every cell a new home for these translucent travelers. they receive messages from yours.

dear clementine of 2010

you are so good. you are so fucking good. and fucking lots of men or fucking a rapper you saw on tv, that doesn't make you bad, beautiful, it doesn't make you bad. i know you love him. your love flows from your fingers, from your lips, from between your legs, from your eyes. i know you work hard at loving him, that you are trying to make yourself lovable because he keeps telling you that there is something wrong with you. there is nothing wrong with you. you are good. all his screaming and all his yelling, all his name calling, you don't deserve it. you are not unworthy of his love. he is unworthy of yours. and i know, it hurts so fucking much because you thought you finally found a place where you belong. you thought he could really love you, through and through, and i know how bad you wanted it. you put up with so much shit to make it true. but it's not true. he doesn't love you. his violence, that's not love. his apologies, that's not love. his excuses, that's not love. even his sweetness and goodness, that's not love. he does not know how. i know you're hurting so much. i know you're trying to put the pieces back together and hide the fact that the whole thing has smashed. i know you've got blood all over you from the shards and i know you are exhausted from the work. and i know that you love him. and you desperately want him to love you too. but he won't. i'm sorry. he won't. he doesn't love you. but i do. i love your small capable hands, your loving smile, your huge fucking heart. i love that you feel the pain of the whole world and that you still try to make it better. i love your ambition, your drive, your creativity, your stubbornness. i love your sense of justice, your sense of humour, your hope. i love your courage, the fact that after everything, after extensive violence, you are still capable of so much love. i love that you went out and claimed your sexuality, after it was stolen from you again and again. i love that you faced down 'slut', 'dyke', 'bitch', 'whore', 'ugly', 'freak', 'nasty scallywag' and that you insisted on your right to your body, expression and pleasure. i love that you learned to ride a bike at 23, that you learned to play guitar and skateboard. you are beautiful and brave. you are who i wanted to be when i grew up, back when we were a little girl. clementine, you have no idea how amazing you are, how beautiful, how pure, how powerful. i know that you don't know how to love yourself yet, that's why you love him so hard. but i want to tell you, you get out. you leave him. you charge that motherfucker and you refuse to ever take on his violence again. i want you to know that you found strength you didn't know existed and you saved your own life. because of you, i have the opportunity to exist. he didn't kill you. you didn't let him. so thank you, thank you for saving my life. in return, i am traveling back in time to find you and tell you that i love you, that it won't hurt this much forever, that he does not deserve you and that you will get away. you are good. believe me. and your life will be so much more than this. love clementine of 2012.

evacuation of stars

stars like tumors taking over my body. i open my mouth as if to speak. i bring my hand to my heart as if, as if i felt anything. i am overcome with stardust, choking on the shit. it is overcome with me, attracted to every crevice, every orifice. oh look, there's the diamond your long term partner left up my asshole. fuck. will i ever redeem myself? would all of you still love me if you knew who you were fucking with? because i'm a bad, bad girl. the glitter begins to bubble, like my body is a cauldron, like i am the grail and out froths eternity, pouring over the top. and my wet lips beg you to take a sip. you want to taste forever and forever you will be mine. i'm so sorry. i let go, but my stars they shine, they shine.

i lay down, crash into the water, it overcomes me, i'm breathing cut rock, sparkling hard and collapsible like air. i am the invention of time, this sparkling girl and i choke and there's blood and i collapse on the floor. is it going to kill me? are you going to kill me for this? because when i left you, yes, the sky did follow me. yes, when i look over my shoulder i can see that the moon is following me. i am not alone even when i try to be.

and you were jealous. jealous that the moon kept following me around, jealous that you could never get me alone, without the presence of the sky. she was always peeking in through the windows, looking, looking for me. and then the ceilings fell in love with me. you declared me crazy. you fucking crazy bitch. you fucking slut. you succubus witch. and i feel the straight jacket and i feel the ice pick and i feel the rope binding my wrists and the stake at my back and the flames that encircle me. i feel the metal instruments searching and prodding inside of me like my grandfather's wet worm tongue. i feel the splitting, the disassembling of my parts.

he touches it and it was me. this is what they do to my body. and i'm up on my broomstick looking down. counting the slashes, the cuts. counting the pushes, the touches, the kisses, the fucks. i keep the inventory of what they do to her, me, what they do to her. i can't breathe. i don't need to. and when they are done, i fly back down and i put her body back together again. i sew her up and kiss her tenderly and she is gushing nothing but stars. the floor is wet with it. the sticky starlight of witches blood. split and sucked and fucked from her. and them drunk like gods from raping a goddess just leave us here to clean up the mess, me and myself.

we put the stars back, the ever multiplying stars. we place them back in her eye sockets, up in her ovaries and piled up in her womb. and even as we are doing this they are multiplying and flying out of her, pouring all over the floor, but we do what we can to try to keep as much as we can inside her. and we seal her with thread and love. i touch her on the head and i don't show her my sadness because it's my job to be the strong one here. but i want to weep. i want to fucking weep. look what they did to her. they split her the fuck open. it's disgusting to see her destroyed like this. but she is resilient. i stroke her. i tell her 'shhh, shhhh' because it's all i can say.

and she isn't crying just slowly gushing starlight and i hold her in my arms until we are strong enough to merge. and then i wake up and i am her and i look at my new healing wounds. i remember that they did this to me and i thank myself for taking care of myself. i stare into the distance where there are stars like my own. i am still multiplying all inside, i am still continuously becoming more than myself, and i know, i know they will kill me for this. i can't stop it. i can't stop it. i mop up the starlight, shake the excess stars from my hair. but there is always more. and for that they will kill her.

the story of my first period

when i got my first period, it was under horrible circumstances. the year was 2000. i was thirteen. i had just graduated from grade eight. that summer, i went with my family to southampton on the shores of lake huron, where my grandma and aunt live and where my mom has a cottage. i met a boy there who became my first boyfriend though we technically never called it that. having been sexually assaulted by my grandfather just the summer before, i felt really emotionally fucked up. i had not been given the opportunity to process and heal from the assault and i had not been protected from further contact with my perpetrator.

i liked this boy i met a lot but i had very ambivalent feelings. i went from feeling totally infatuated with him to feeling very trapped and scared, and then angry. he felt me up under the blankets when we were sitting on the couch watching a movie with his little brother and my little sister sitting there on the same couch. i did not want him to do that, because they were in the room, but he gave me no way to say no without exposing what he was doing. so i let him do it and it was very confusing for me. i enjoyed the sensation of his hands on my breasts but i also felt violated, angry, horrified.

i was very hot and cold with him. and then, the night before i had to leave southampton he gave me a bracelet with his name on the one side and mine on the other. and then he snuck over to my grandma's place in the middle of the night, where i was staying in this little shed on the yard we call the bunkhouse. i wanted him to leave and i tried everything i knew to get him to go without directly telling him. but he cornered me into having my first 'real' kiss, besides my grandfather the summer before. i ended up awkwardly telling him that i didn't like kissing because my first kiss was from my grandfather. when he left, i was so glad and i went inside and cried my eyes out. part of me thought i was 'in love' with him, but i was happy to be away from him because i just could not deal with the whole thing.

so then, after my family left southampton we went to coe hill, where we spent pretty much every august and lots more time besides that, to a little cottage on a little lake which belongs to my dad's parents. this was where my pedophile grandfather would prey on me, my sister and my girl cousins. so we were there. back where he'd made out with me the summer before.

in the middle of the night i woke up with extreme pain in my stomach. i didn't know why it hurt so much. i thought maybe i had to take a shit or something and i went to the washroom. but i didn't have to. and the pain just wouldn't stop. i didn't want to take tylenol because i heard that would make stomach aches worse. so i sat up in pain for a long time, really freaking out and not understanding why i was in so much pain, but too embarrassed to say anything to anyone. finally i decided to just take a tylenol just in case it might work. and eventually the pain subsided and i went to sleep (in a room with nothing but a yellow curtain separating me from where my pedophile grandfather slept).

in the morning there was bright red blood in my underwear. it was a shocking shade of red and i thought i had cut myself somehow. i knew what a period was, but that did not even occur to me, because it was so bright and unlike the brown period stains i had seen. i thought i must have hurt myself somehow. a kid in my school had recently had internal bleeding and i thought maybe this was happening to me. my stomach had hurt so much last night, it made sense to me. i was pretty scared but way too embarrassed to say anything, or ask for help. i panicked in silence. i think it was that night that i eventually recognized what was happening to me. i was getting my first period.

the next day, the 'boyfriend' from earlier that summer showed up. my aunt brought him and his little brother to coe hill. he looked horrible. he had bleached his hair in a way that i thought looked horrible. i didn't want him there. i didn't want him to touch me and i knew he was going to try. i was bleeding my first blood, caught there between a twelve year old boy and an old old man, both who laid claim to my body, who thought it was theirs to touch and feel and probe and prod as they desired. and me, inside my body, possessing it, bleeding my first blood, resisting.

i went outside that night. left the 'boyfriend' and my grandfather and my family inside the little cottage lit up with yellow light. i went outside into the cool sweet moonlight. i walked to the tree. i threw my arms around her and i kissed her and i held her pulsing body close to mine. and i celebrated and i grieved and i gathered strength. i knew i was not alone. i knew She was with me. my faith was strong. i bled and held that beautiful strong tree, alone in the moonlight and that was mine. that they couldn't take from me.

your own

let me tell you a secret. you have everything you need. you are wise. you are brave. you are resilient. you are capable. and there is no one else like you. you are worthy of love and respect. you are a manifestation of the divine. your life is your own and no one else's. this information has been purposefully hidden from you, distorted, refuted, covered over. but it is an inalienable, unalterable truth. you have the right to claim your destiny, to feel your feelings, to speak your truth. you have the right to set your boundaries, to explore your desires, to discover and become who you are. you have the right to change your mind, to come to your own conclusions, to honour your own wisdom. whatever lies you are told, whatever suffering you are made to endure, keep this in your heart and keep it safe. you are your own.

a bicycle ride to the end of the world

cut the pieces, pull the insides out. my insides are bleeding, out. my love affair with myself gone rotten and stale because i refused to ask the right questions and then i refused to answer them. but now i remember who i am. broken sentences hanging dead. cold like that. fragmented. cut. the pieces get smaller and smaller until there is nothing left. just texture and truth telling caught somewhere in the lies. remember, when the lights were off and no one could see you. remember the dead trees in the water not unlike ghosts. still. steady. weighted. not unlike chains. wasting away, awaiting the belated return. desire, that fire, sweet elixir, lights up like branches, glowing steady sweet and throbbing, erased. erased. i felt nothing. i felt absolutely nothing. now how can i even know what i like or why i like it? this pleasure at being fucked, when i liked being fucked, was a pleasure in my femininity, or was it?

all i know is that i was taking women's studies and sexuality studies courses and getting abused by my boyfriend and really, there came a point when he was fucking me and i couldn't stand it, i couldn't fucking stand his condomless dick just fucking and fucking and having no idea what it feels like for me. there came a point when i was like *if your dick is in my vagina for one second longer i'm gonna fucking puke.* except i didn't say that. i didn't say anything. *i'm way too fucking full and i'm going to fucking puke. get your dick away from me. get it the fuck away from me.* except i didn't say that. i didn't say anything. i just lied there in the dark like a fucking corpse bathed in blue light, my body some kind of mannequin, some kind of sweet plastic doll, some kind of fantasy, wife, hooker/whore, daughter...

who am i this time? this time i am your wife and your prisoner. this time my devotion is real. this time the map is a bicycle trail that takes us out to the forest and i travel along it and everything is green, i feel safe here. i feel safe here. i open my eyes and he is still fucking me. i'm not sure if i'm still crying. i'm not sure if i like it. if this is what love is, somehow, because we had a picnic by the rocks, by the water, and i was topless in the heat of summer and we loved each other. remember. we loved each other. so how did it get to this? what happened? was it ever real? but i think it was. i loved you. riding my bicycle, you riding yours, i had never been happier in my entire life and i didn't need to party and i didn't need the booze, i had you baby. i had you. i know what happened to you so i rationalized your violent behaviour away. but i should have stopped it so much sooner. i should have known it couldn't stay better, it always had to get worse. and then so much worse than that. and then more fucked up than we could have imagined, when it started, when we drank beer in the alleyway, before you were arrested, before i even quit drinking, and it was simple and we didn't know we would love each other and we didn't know we would lose

part three: rupture

part four: yes i am a slut

yes i am a slut

yes i am a slut. because i have big tits that pour out of pretty much every shirt. because i like to show them off. because i used to charge 200 an hour and sometimes i would come and my client wouldn't cuz that's how much i was into fucking. because i've had trains run on me. because i liked it. because in grade eight a boy pulled down my shirt and bra in front of the whole class and my teacher and everyone saw my nipples. because he got a slap on the wrist and i was told by the principal that it was partially my fault because of the shirt i was wearing. because after that i started showing my tits to guys cuz i figured i was used goods. because when i was nineteen and being assaulted by a bunch of guys for not shaving my armpits they felt the need to pull my tits out of my shirt. because when i was twelve my grandfather forcibly made out with me. yes i am a slut. because i love sucking dick and i'll take his load all over my face and tits and in my mouth. because i used to get drunk and fuck random guys all the time even on weeknights. because i'm bisexual and everyone assumes bisexuals are slutty even when we're in monogamous relationships. because i'm a femme queer grrrl and everyone thinks femme queer grrrls are just 'doing it for attention' and are accessible to men. because the first time i was kissed in a way i actually like my girlfriend and i were told we were disgusting and going to burn in hell. yes i am a slut. because i fucked my boyfriend in the ass with my strap on. because i used to work in a sex shop. because i love the night. because i wear miniskirts. because i flirt. because i've gone to bars by myself. because i've pissed in alleyways. because sometimes i like sex. because sometimes i don't like sex. because i've been raped. because i'm a feminist. because i'm a survivor. because i'm a cum guzzling nympho. because i own sex toys. lots of them. because the only person who can make me come is myself and i'm fine with that. because i rub my clit when i'm being fucked. because i've done webcam work. because i've posed naked for pictures. because i like to masturbate. because i've always loved to masturbate. because i used to jerk off to naked pictures of women when i was like ten years old and i thought there was something seriously wrong with me. because there is nothing wrong with me. yes i am a slut. because my boyfriend called me one. because he got on top of me and screamed it in my face. because he called me it on my birthday. because random men have yelled slut at me more times than i could possibly count if i tried to sit down and write a list. because i have been called an ugly bitch, sweetheart, honey and other degrading names more times than i could count too. because i've been called a dyke and told to shave my armpits and my pussy and told to lose weight and told to shut up and told to say yes to my pedophile grandfather. because i am sick of being told and this time i am telling you. yes i am a slut. because my pussy is beautiful and insatiable. because i love my body. because the clothes i'm most comfortable in apparently make me a target for rape. because when i was raped i was in my bed at home. because my body belongs to me no matter how many times i've been violated and none of it was my fault ever. yes i am a slut. because yes, i do fucking know what the word means and yes i am a feminist and yes i am intelligent and yes i do choose to say yes i am a slut. because the police officer who said women should stop dressing like sluts to avoid being victimized was talking about me and he was talking about you and he was talking about all of us. and because if we say it's okay to rape any of us then it's okay to rape all of us. because the slut card can be pulled out at any time and you never know when it will be used against you. because it can always be used against you, even if you've tried hard to make the 'right' choices. because all of us are sluts because in a rape culture women are considered inherently rapable. because none of us can be free of the word until those of us who choose to are free to embrace the word. because the word will never lose its power to hurt as long as we allow them to control it. because i respect a person's right to self identify and expect the same respect in return. because i am taking a cue from my queer sisters who helped in the reclamation of words like queer and dyke, words that mean so much to our history and struggle. yes i am a slut. yes it is a complicated identity full of disempowerment, empowerment, struggle and resistance. yes it was forced on me and used against me and yes i and many of us were able to find different, new and empowering ways of relating to the word. yes we are sluts. so please hear us out. hear what we have to say. don't condescendingly tell us whether or not we are sluts or whether or not we can find empowerment this way. yes we can, yes we do, yes we are.

fuck the future fuck the past

that's the way sex is supposed to be. you were late. i'd already fallen asleep. but i jumped out of bed when you said you were downstairs. ran and got you, put you in my bed. beautiful. i get so shy and awkward around you, even after five years. but tonight, i just went for it. just took what's mine. kissing you. sucking on your sweet lips. the smell of you. my eyes on you. pressing my body next to you, shirts coming off so we can feel our skin pressing hot against each other. just for this moment, i don't want to move. i just want to hold you. i let my mind shut off. i think no thoughts. i just feel your breath and mine entwining. i see your eyes, looking at my lips, watching. we're naked. your body, your strong arms. i'm on top of you, straddling you, looking at you, kissing you. sucking your neck, making you shudder, biting your shoulders. i let myself follow my own pleasure. i allow myself to enjoy you. the boundaries of our bodies are blurring through the motion and the movement and the wetness, the combining of you and i. both of us losing it, losing track of words. your dick is inside of me and i'm fucking you and i can't stop, you hold me there, press me close, call me by my real name. i follow the motions of my body, unable to stop chasing down the pleasure as i collapse into orgasm, the pure sensation of us together causing ripples all through me, i come on top of you. you hold me. i kiss you. your dick outside of me again, the separateness. we close the distance. my tongue in your mouth, licking each other, coaxing each other, speaking in a language long before words. and we talk and we laugh. you ask me what i'm thinking, you say "past, present or future?" and i say "present, definitely present" and you laugh. you say "yeah, fuck the future and fuck the past" and i put your dick in my mouth and you put your head back. and i'm sucking you now, devouring your dick, feeling nothing but devotion for the pleasure you invoke within me. i repay the favour. i suck your dick so lovingly. i take it into my throat, i swallow the whole thing, i suck on the head, enjoying every moment, every reaction in your face and body. you pull my ass on to you and put my pussy in your face, pulling my clit into your mouth. we suck each other off, locked in pleasure, sensation and texture. feeling and being with one another. i can feel the folds of my pussy being sucked into the warmth of your mouth, your beautiful hands squeezing my ass, pulling me into you. your dick down my throat, we find a rhythm, lost in motion. then you move me forward, put the condom on, and situate me reverse cowgirl on your dick and i work it for you, as you enjoy the view, smacking my ass. i fuck you diligently, working on the motion, giving you what you deserve. my vagina fucking your dick, pulling the pleasure from it. until you can't take it anymore and you flip me over and push your dick into me and fuck. i grab you, pull you close, suck your skin and bite your shoulders as you ride me through your orgasm. i hold you while you twitch and shiver, refusing the space, enjoying the completeness. and we lie there for a moment, completely entangled, kissing each other, speechless. and when you are putting your clothes on, i come up behind you and wrap my arms around you and you stop what you're doing and press my arms into your chest. we say things to each other with our bodies that we don't know how to say with words. and this is love. we are loving each other.

spillllll over

i'm not who i was. i'm not yet who i'm going to be. i don't have it in me to make sense right now. i don't have it in me to take my fucked up life and turn it into an inspiring and empowering story for you. i don't have it in me to answer all the questions that get asked of me because i have turned myself into a public figure. i don't have it in me to explain my art, to explain the intricacies, to explain where the love became pain, where the pain became love, to explain which fucking i wanted and which i didn't, and which felt good and which did not and which is empowering and feminist and which makes me a sad, broken girl. and i don't have it in me to explain about compulsive sexuality in a world that punishes me for any sexuality, and i don't know how to tell you i haven't had a dick in my pussy for more than a month because i don't want a pat on the back and i don't want you to think this means i've 'cleaned up my act'. i don't want to hear about love and sweet touching and looking into each other's eyes and lovers in the spring time. i don't want people telling me how damaged i am and that i need professional help. i'm full of professional help, the good and the bad. i don't want to be a role model or an example, i don't want to be a thesis statement or the proof of someone else's point. i don't want to justify any of it. it's my body. the things i've done, the things i did not do. the things i've felt, the things i wanted. i don't have it in me to explain. there are no easy answers. this is all a process. and i am showing you all my process because that's what i want to do. but that does not make it a free for all and it does not mean that my sex life is up for discussion and debate. i know. i talk about it all the time. i'm such a slut. blablabla. and i am. and i was. and i have. and it's all true. and i also have a lover who i've never fucked and never even wanted to. and i also couldn't have an orgasm from about seventeen to eighteen, despite being orgasmic my whole childhood. and, and, and. not just or. and no, you can't cite my sexual partners in your footnotes and no, you can't define these experiences for me. they are mine. and my interpretations of them are multiple because reality is multiplistic and things can be both empowering and disturbing, both liberating and oppressive, both freeing and trapping at the same fucking time. i am not a poster girl for sexual liberation nor i am i sad, sad story about what happens when children are sexually abused. my promiscuity is linked to my trauma and guess what, so were my long, codependent monogamous relationships. but i don't ever hear 'you were sexually abused as a child, are you sure you're not just using romance to cope?' i only ever hear about the sex and how the sex must be fucked up because i am, and it is, it has been. but no one-night-stand ever put me through the drywall, no one-night-stand ever fucked me night after night while i laid there like a dead fish. and yeah, one-night-stands have done violent fucked up shit too. and one-night-stands have been fucking lovely. and it's been all. not either/or. and i want to be able to just spill my guts and say it's all true without having to defend and explain. yes, i have issues with compulsive sexuality, trauma, lack of self worth. yes, i have fucked guys when really i just wanted them to talk to me. i have also talked to guys when i really just wanted them to fuck me. and i have laughed at jokes that are not funny. i don't have all the answers. nor do i want to have them. i am a twenty five year old recovering addict, i have ptsd, i am a survivor and a feminist and have in the past been a nympho and have in the past had no interest in sex. and right now, i just want people to be nice to me instead of expecting that i will explain it all to them and make it simple and make it clear. it's not simple. it's not clear. and you are going to have to do your own thinking and there is no one truth to arrive at, there are many, many, many. yes i liked it. no i did not. it is too easy to fall back on the slut shaming script, it is too easy to say 'oh you were sexually abused so that's why you are promiscuous'. it is too easy and it's also just plain mean. you sound like my abusive ex who called me a slut consistently, who i loved dearly and was completely and utterly faithful to. it is also too easy to say that sex is this totally empowering and uncomplicated thing for clementine, because it is not and i don't think i've ever made it seem so. i am a rape victim and a rape survivor. my first kiss was forced on me by my grandfather. i have sincerely enjoyed things that many would consider inherently degrading. these things are not cause/effect and neither are they unrelated. i don't have the answers but i clearly do and maybe if you watch the motions you will see an unfolding, but in the meantime please remember that i am a human being.

masturbation and me

i have always touched my vulva for as long as i can remember because it's a natural way to get to know the body. this touching was nice but it did not lead to sexual pleasure. i'm not sure at what age, maybe eight or so, i was in a bathtub that had jets. i turned to the side and by accident the jet stream hit my clit. i was amazed at the sensation and immediately hooked. i started my lifelong practice of masturbation.

i don't remember when it initially donned on me that what i was doing was wrong and shameful, but it did. i think it's a combination of living in a culture that treats women like sexual objects and denies their pleasure (children pick up on these messages too) and the fact that i was being sexually abused by my grandfather and therefore saw sexuality as icky and scary. i believed fundamentally, to my core, that what i was doing was shameful and that i should stop. but it felt so damn good.

i would go long periods where i would refuse to allow myself to masturbate. then i would give in and go on a masturbation binge. i had such a high sex drive as a child. i enjoyed rubbing my clit and penetrating my vagina with small objects like a toothbrush handle.

at about the age of ten/eleven the internet came into existence. i was a weirdo and a loner so i naturally loved the internet. there was a website called 'ex pages' that was like this really super simple way to make your own webpage. i naturally made my own webpage. one day, while attempting to access ex pages, i typed the address in wrong and ended up at a porn site. it was images of naked women posing, no men. i was immediately extremely turned on and went off and masturbated. and then later, i came back to the site again, and again.

this made things much, much worse. i was already deeply ashamed of masturbation. but this? i was looking at naked *women*. i was a girl. i knew that this was not appropriate and acceptable behaviour. i had zero access to representations of queerness, besides a gay uncle and a lesbian couple who were friends of my mom. but i did not consider myself to be 'like them'. i felt like a total freak. but i was so utterly turned on by images of women's bodies.

masturbation was my deep, dark secret. there was no way i was going to tell a single person. there was no way. and i, clementine morrigan, did not admit to a single person that i masturbate until the age of seventeen. well, a single person in 'real life'. but the internet was a different story.

the internet was different in those days. facebook certainly did not exist. everything was way more anonymous. profiles did not include pictures. i frequented a website for girls called gurl.com and there, on that site, there was a masturbation message board. this board was my saviour. while i could not believe for a second that any of my female classmates and friends masturbated i found that there were other 'freaks' like me. in fact, there were lots of them. the board acted as a community where we talked about our desires and fantasies and shared masturbation tips and tricks. girls started sharing erotica on the board and gurl.com shut it down, because it was adult material on a site for young girls.

by grade six all the boys in my class openly talked about masturbation. it was seen as a normal thing for guys to do. but female masturbation was taboo and no girl would ever dare suggest that she took part in such a thing. in grade eight, a boy in my class asked me to let him see my hand. thinking he was flirting with me, i offered up my right hand. he said 'is that the hand you write with?' i said no, and offered up my dominant left hand. he smelled it. and he announced to everyone that it smelled like fish, proof that i masturbated.

i was utterly mortified. because it was true. i did masturbate. and i believed him. i thought he really could smell my vulva (i realize now that he was fucking with me) and i felt like my dirty secret had been totally exposed. i was so ashamed and embarrassed. i denied it adamantly. but him and the other boys insisted. my hand smelled like fish so i must have been touching myself.

after that, i scrubbed my hands raw after i masturbated. convinced that the smell had some super staying power. i started putting plastic bags over my hands when i touched myself so that no one would know. when i think back on this now, i am so disturbed that i was made to feel so deeply ashamed for such a natural, healthy behaviour.

when i was fifteen i started having sex. it pretty much sucked. it didn't feel anything like the sexual pleasure i had been inducing in myself for years. i didn't understand why. i thought vaginal penetration was supposed to feel miraculous. i felt defective that my own hand did it for me better than my boyfriend. he started to be concerned that i wasn't coming, so i started faking it. i faked it hardcore for three months and then finally admitted i was faking it. i started rubbing my clit during sex, became orgasmic and continue to do so to this day.

i finally started to admit to masturbation at the age of seventeen, living on my own in toronto, attending a queer alternative school. in queer, sex-positive environments i came to understand that masturbation is an amazing and really healthy activity, physically, spiritually and emotionally. i dropped the dead weight of my shame and began to revel in my body. i had been my own lover for years and years and i was finally not ashamed of it.

unfortunately, sexual violence intervened and made me unable to orgasm, even by myself, for a year. that's another story for another time, but suffice to say i eventually found my way back to myself.

masturbation continued to be a regular and healthy part of my sex life into my adult years. i generally masturbated several times a day. i saw it as a way to keep in touch with myself, communicate with myself, care for myself, reduce stress and explore my desires. i did research and learned about my sexual anatomy. i felt good about it.

a few months into a relationship with a guy who i thought was amazing and who i was madly in love with (who turned out to be incredibly abusive, and this should have been a red flag) masturbation came up. by this point, i was used to telling boyfriends that i masturbate and i was used to them thinking it was sexy. my boyfriend and i lived together. he had gone to bed and i was showering. i jerked off in the shower. i later told him about it, thinking he would think it was hot. he got mad at me. he asked me why i didn't come into the bedroom and have sex with him. i told him i hadn't been in the mood for sex. i just wanted a quickie with myself before bed. he told me that if he really sexually satisfied me i shouldn't masturbate. i gave up masturbating for the rest of my relationship with him.

i became incredibly sexually disconnected with myself. and i am still working to reestablish my sexual relationship with myself. but i am back to masturbating daily, i am pleased to let you know.

the reason i am writing all of this is because female masturbation is still a taboo topic and i'm sure there are many girls and women out there who can relate to my story. i want to let you know you are not alone, you are not a freak and there is nothing shameful about masturbation. masturbation is the safest sex act you can take part in. it is an act of self care and self love. it reduces stress, increases circulation and improves your relationship with yourself. in short, masturbation is good for you. if it's something you enjoy doing, that's fuckin great. and, in this culture which shames female sexuality and objectifies female bodies, you should be really fuckin proud of yourself for maintaining any kind of sexual relationship with yourself.

no matter your age, your sexual orientation, what you look like, your gender, your relationship status, etc, you can masturbate if you want to and you can feel fuckin good about it. seriously.

brb. i have a date with my hitatchi magic wand.

bad skin: a psoriatic manifesto

what happened to your elbows? what is that? do you have eczema? ow, did you fall? does that hurt? is that contagious? what is that? were you attacked by mosquitoes? did you fall skateboarding? what's psoriasis? have you tried adjusting your diet? have you tried this new miracle cream that i heard about on the radio? have you tried shea butter? does that hurt? what happened? what is that?

or, without words, the look. the look that falls on my elbows, my red and flaking, peeling skin. the hesitation in their eyes as i watch them try to decide if they should say something. but they want to know. they are itching to know. why does my skin look so different from their own? why is my skin a bright red scream, an interruption of the flawless scenery? why are my elbows so brazenly exposed? why don't i fix that somehow, or hide it from sight? why am i not ashamed? why don't i make it go away?

what is it about my body that makes it look like that? they need to understand it and define it because it scares them. their reaction is immediate. their eyes start and their lips finish it. they want me in my place, labeled, judged and understood. they need an explanation. they need to know. what it is. why it's like that. why it's not hidden from sight.

bad skin. bad because it's like a stone in the machine. bad because it's an interruption, an imposition of my imperfection onto this perfect scene. bad because it's a reminder that not all bodies function the same, not all skin is produced at the same rate. bad because it is a reminder of pain. bad because it's right there and it won't go away. bad because it's visible when it should be hidden or at least carried with shame. bad because it's a problem, don'tyouknow, and should be fixed. bad because it's not okay just the way it is.

bad as in unruly, untamed. bad as in *fuck you, my body is absolutely okay.* bad as in *i am not an object for your consumption.* bad as in *it's none of your fucking business.* bad as in *i am not ashamed.*

my body functions differently than yours does. my body looks different than yours does. i do not owe you an explanation for it. especially when i don't even know you. your invasive questions, your staring eyes, your inability to handle my 'bad' skin, these say more about you than they do about me. they tell me that you are invested in an illusion of normal, same bodies. they tell me that difference alarms you, that the unknown disturbs you and that you can only regain your composure through labeling, invading, conquering and knowing. my offensive skin must be explained, not only what it is and why it is but also why it's there, in your face, visible and seen. you must know why i have not discovered a miracle cure, changed my diet, gone on immune system suppressing pills that could kill me but hey — i would have good skin.

your questions and your looking, they are a violence. they are an attempt to force my unruly body back into a tamed state. they are a demand that i disappear or at the very least explain myself. how dare i walk around with my peeling, red skin, acting like i'm normal, just as human as you. and you might scoff at this and say they are just innocent questions, just curious looks. but the suicide rate for those of us who develop severe psoriasis speaks for itself. we are not killing ourselves because our skin is flaking. we are killing ourselves because you can't handle the flakes.

devour

out of the broken pieces i will make something more beautiful than you could have imagined or willed. out of the shattered fragments that you smashed out of the whole, i will build myself an idol, to praise the Crone. out of my bodies, the one that you loved and the one that you broke, i will make one creature, a living girl with all her parts and then some. i will create myself in Her image, with both Wings and Horns, with both Breasts and Bird Feet. i will not be the milk you drink, i will wander the desert, barren and dried up, for more than a thousand years. and like a mother bitch exhausted from her nursing pups, i will be utterly relieved to be free of your suckling. i am an oasis, a spring, an endless well, but no you may not drink from my waters anymore. i refuse. out of the nothingness, the endlessness that i endlessly considered i found the form of the Universe, i saw Her intention, Her Sacred Will. and i walk through the gateways of Hell, through the Sacredness of Deaths and Endings, i walk through the murder, degradation, humiliation, shaming and erasure of the Goddess, i walk through and i come through Alive. like Her, you could not kill me. like Her, i have conquered Death. and now Death belongs to me. i am Eve, blood in my teeth, the Serpent, She told me to Eat. Devour. i am the endlessness, i am the nothingness, the number eight turned on its side, infinity. you cannot kill me. hysterical, feverish, i can feel the Sacred Madness and i walk into it. we are all invited by the Goddesses. they call our names in the endless pulse of the Universe and i follow the Light and the Darkness. i follow the emptiness that is full of nothingness and everything there is or ever could be. do you believe me? will you come with me? are you afraid? are you afraid that we are all going to Die? that Hell shall swallow the Earth? swallow, suck, the endless gaping vagina dentata, the Earth Herself will Suck us up. Devour. i Eat. the fruit of this whole world, my eyes are opened, i leave the garden, i wander through the deserts and find my Barren Sister, the Sacred Crone. i love Her, i am Her, we taste the Fruit, she tells us, commands us, implores us to Eat.

O

shine, the size of open eyes, the disk reflects the light and fills the sky and i — my mouth is open, forming O, there is no question there? an open window. a door, a front door, left wide open in the middle of the night. there are strange people sleeping in my house. and i think there always have been. and that's a very unsettling thought. so i look behind the shower curtain and under the staircase... this is where they keep them, where they hide? shine, i see the night seeping out of the cup like black blood and yes it disturbs me a little bit. my limbs twitch. i begin to wonder. i shake the feeling no. i dig my fingers inside of no, O. the open hole. we walk like endless legs and swim like we never had them. we walk and we wake like it is nothing and so i stand, separated from them, becoming another one and another one and each time i get further away. there will be nothing left. i will be too far away, just a dot, just an O, oh, oh, ohhh. zero. take the place of nothingness. make it stand for something (else). O. her mouth took the shape of an O? was that a question? her eyes looked so shocked and i didn't want to mention. so tell me, what was she doing with her mouth like that? shine, shine. the moon, globe, white disk, tonight it's bigger than ever. the black blood in the toilet bowl. oh. it escapes my lips. oh no. i wonder. i wander? i take the tour of veins back to the centre. but it is endless. tell me so. tell me, no, no. i form the words, the vowels slip like jewels, they sparkle but they are pointless, oh, oh. oh. uncanny, left without the whole, an unstellated star, a star without its points. so tell me so. shine, bright and slow. the white light of the full moon, lunacy, sweet but oh? O.

the girl with the red hair really needs to shave her fucking armpits

there is a picture of me from when i'm eleven years old. i'm in my bathing suit on a floating dock with my sister and my brother. under my armpits you can see long armpit hair. my armpit hair was brand new then. it's a beautiful picture. i look so beautiful. it's so fucked to think how much drama that hair would bring.

i love my armpit hair. i liked it when it first grew there too. i liked the feel of it. but i knew that i'd be made fun of for it. i knew without question. so, at the prospect of going swimming with my friends, i went into the bathroom and picked up a shaving razor i found in there. i ran it over my armpits without soap or water because i was eleven years old and i didn't know how shaving worked. i cut myself and bled but i got rid of most of the hair. that's when i started shaving. i had to shave every day if my armpits were going to be exposed. stubble seemed to come back really fast. my armpits were always sore and red and full of little irritation bumps because i shaved so much. i went through periods where i just didn't shave but at these times i always covered my armpits.

years passed. i went through a lot of shit. i moved to toronto at the age of sixteen and pretty much immersed myself in the queer scene. it was there, as a dyke, that i first gained the confidence and courage to show off my hairy armpits. i would go months without shaving and wear little dresses and give the finger to people who stared. i dated a girl who didn't shave her armpits either. i became aware of just how shocking it was to people. people literally do a double take. i raised my hand to answer a question in school and the whole class burst out laughing. this has happened to me in different classes.

there was a boy i liked and i wanted to impress him in that hetero-normative way. so whenever i'd see him (which wasn't that often) i'd shave my armpits. i felt like i was betraying myself. i felt weird. i didn't like the look of my bare naked armpits but i was scared of what he might say or think if he saw my natural hair.

shortly after i turned seventeen i tried to kill myself. but i realized that i didn't want to die. i realized my life was pretty fucked up and i had to start being honest with myself about how i really felt, about everything. no more bullshit, or at least, i wanted to start on the path to no more bullshit. i didn't want to be unhappy anymore. i wanted to be loved for who i am, not for who i can pretend to be. i stopped shaving my armpits and haven't shaved them since.

i continued to experience harassment and jokes about my armpit hair but it didn't faze me too much. i was confident in my body and sexuality. my armpit hair felt like a representation of my sexuality, my lust, my womanhood. i think it's really sexy. and i knew other people did too, they were just scared. scared because female armpit hair is totally erased from western cultural imagination. it seemed to people that i was doing this on purpose, causing the hair to grow, rather than simply choosing not to remove it. there were times when i felt really embarrassed when i was made to be a laughingstock, but it didn't stop me. i felt so comfortable in my skin.

when i was nineteen i went to a local show with my sister. i was dancing around and acting crazy, and i was the only girl doing so. i was wearing a tanktop. the singer in the band said into the mic "the girl with the red hair (me) really needs to shave her fucking armpits".

people were laughing at me. people were throwing shit at me. i was giving these people the finger and raising my arm, showing off the hair. then a guy punched me in the face, knocking my glasses off. i tried to hit him back but another guy caught my arm and restrained me. i was pushed, shoved and hit by a group of guys. my shirt was pulled down during all of this. my sister's arms were restrained. i was dragged out on my back by my pigtails, down some stairs and my head was smashed into a pole along the way. it was fucked up and very, very traumatizing. nothing like that had ever happened to me before. after that people would pass the store i worked at in the mall and shout 'shave your armpits!' at me while i was working.

i didn't pick up a razor though. fuck it. i know who i am and i can't pretend to be anyone else. i love the curl of hair under my arms. i love the sweat smell that lingers there. i love running my fingers through it. fuck the haters. fuck them. i really hope i don't get beaten up again. but i'm not going to shave my fuckin armpits.

she did her makeup on the subway

we walked in the snow, inappropriately dressed, high on weed and teenage love and we were so cold. we went behind an apartment building and found a vent with hot air coming out and we warmed ourselves there. she reminded me that i was still living and she taught me how to let go. she wore elaborate outfits and did her makeup on the subway and fed the pigeons wherever she went. they came to her in flocks and people glared at her thinking "don't feed the birds" but she didn't care. she loved to feed them and everyone. she loved to give food. she defended me and she loved me and she protected me. i loved her and she left me for a boy. my heart splintered into a million pieces and i left the city and in some ways i never came back.

buttercups

i'm pulling yellow buttercups still on their stem right out of my right nostril. they must have been embedded in my brain. they must have been in there for some time. i take a breath. it's like hearing the fullness of sound. i didn't know i wasn't quite breathing all this time. i didn't know that there were flowers blocking the passageway to my brain. i didn't know that i didn't know what i was doing. i thought i was so wise, then. i thought i'd been given the greatest gift and i thought i deserved it. now i'm looking at these perfect flowers in my hand, still alive, and so am i. it's so strange what we can survive. the crushing defeat that i never wanted to experience let alone live through. it's behind me now. the grass is littered with tiny yellow flowers, delicate and full of colour, robust with colour, unbreakable in their intensity. and he's not with me here, he's not holding my hand. i pulled the flowers out of my brain and stared at them. he's not here to see them. he's not here to say h*ow strange, that you could live with flowers in your brain.* buttercups, no less. fucking perfect. and i sigh that heavy, bewildered sigh that lovers sigh when love has died. i strain my eyes, looking for the details, promises of something yet to unfold. it's so good to be alone. to not have to try so hard to be your girl

revictimization

my body speaks in silences, in spaces, in what it feels and does not feel. what i cannot feel. unfortunately there has been much violence here. much pushing and pulling, much aching, much containing. i have taken what i have taken. i have endured. my body speaks to me and asks me please to stop, to set a boundary. i can't keep freezing. i'm freezing. it's what i know but it simply continues the pain. i lie in the tent on my back and pretend to be asleep as he feels me up and i hate it. why am i allowing this? because i don't know how to make it stop. i am so afraid of my own no. so afraid it won't be listened to anyway, so what is the use?

i don't want to be touched anymore. i need a fucking break. i don't want to be called pretty and sexy. i don't want to be reminded of my fuckability. i need a break. i am tired. and if i make it back, if i ever find my way back to my own pleasure, my own desire, i need it to be something different. i can no longer find vicarious pleasure in knowing that he wants to fuck me, i can no longer pretend that i am him fucking me. i have to find my way back into my body, the body i have been separated from.

revictimization. yes. i didn't want to make things worse. i didn't know the way out. i thought i was taking another path but i was just following the same one in circles. i was just doing what i know. but my body still speaks, still tells me. there is that feeling in my gut that i have ignored. i won't ignore it anymore.

part five: strange girls have feelings too

NOT
FUCKING
INTERESTED

DIRTY PUNK ROCK WITCH

WHAT I DO WITH MY BODY IS
NONE OF YOUR FUCKING BUSINESS

FREE SAFE ACCESSIBLE RESPECTFUL
ABORTION FOR ANYONE WHO WANTS IT

FIERCE FEMMES FUCK SHIT UP

NOT YOUR WIFE
NOT YOUR GIRL
NOT YOUR BITCH

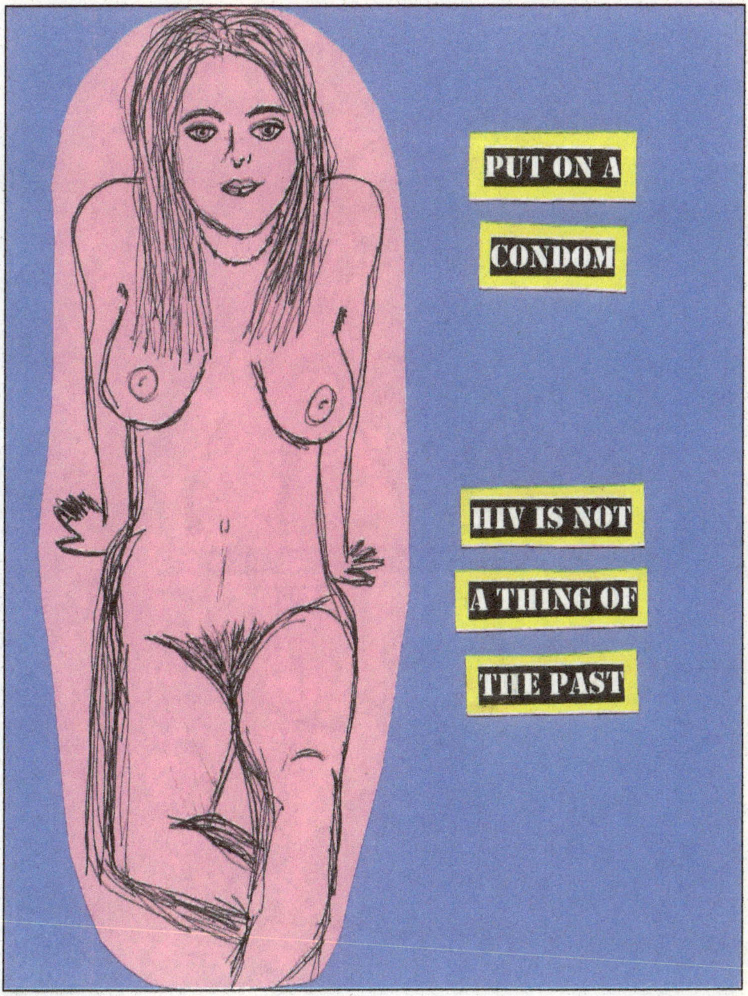
PUT ON A
CONDOM
HIV IS NOT
A THING OF
THE PAST

STRANGE GIRLS HAVE FEELINGS TOO

FEMMES:
CAPABLE
OF
FUCKING
YOUR
BRAINS
OUT

MY BODY
BELONGS
TO ME

part six: better for it

walking home

i'm walking down the street. i see the eyes of passerby's scanning, staring, stopping at my breasts. my breasts. i glance down and yes, there they are. this shirt isn't even low cut. but yeah, they are there, undeniable. i walk past this guy and he says "i like your hair" and i say "thanks" and he says "i like your shirt" and i say "thanks" and he says "i like your chest". i say nothing. there is nothing left to say. why must my body, which i am and which i love, be turned into a cage? why must i be forced to be nothing but my body? the way he is looking at me makes me feel like shit. i am walking down the street, feeling connected to the trees and all of humanity and i am smiling at those who pass me and now i feel like shit. i don't want to be reduced to my body. his eyes linger, linger on my breasts. he mutters "sexy" and the next guy half a block down says "i like the way you look" and then after him a guy winks at me. it's getting later and darker and it's summer so i'm wearing a tubetop and the words of the canadian judge who declared that a woman was not 'really' raped because she was wearing a tubetop and therefore 'sex was in the air' echo in my ears. and i think i'm fine, i'm wearing running shoes, and if not, it's just one quick motion for my keys or my phone and i'm weighing out which would be better to go for first and i consider the distance to the nearest busy intersection and i consider what i would do if he had a knife. i hear keys jingling behind me. a man walking at a slow pace and no one around in this neighborhood now except me and him. so i slow right down and let him pass me. he seems reluctant to. i'd rather keep him in my view. i'm fine. i'm fine now. and i'm walking, confident. my strong legs and my eyes clear ahead of me. and then a car pulls up beside me with the window rolled down and the guy inside asks me if i want a ride. i shake my head. no. no, i don't. i don't want to be perpetually seen as at risk of rape, i don't want to have to think about this shit. and are you hoping for a blowjob too? because i know it is not kindness in the tone of your voice. more like hope. my feet keep moving. my breasts are still there. i am still human despite the way all these uninvited looks make me feel. i am still human and this body is what i get around in, it is not here to make your dick hard. i do not exist to be looked at. i do not exist for you.

sexual violence is not sexy: reimagining masculinities and what it means to be a man

men:

i don't hate you and you know that so please don't even say it. we don't need to go down that road. i have listened to too many of your stories, stared into too many of your eyes, i have sucked too many dicks and loved it, learned too much wisdom and gained too much friendship to write men off. if i hated you i would just say fuck it. there's no way i would spend so much time negotiating all this sexist bullshit.

so now that we've got that out of the way and you know that i'm coming from a place of love, i have to say this.

you can face yourself and you don't have to be ashamed. it takes more courage and more strength to say no to a power that comes from domination and humiliation than it does to take part in it. i know that there is a part of you that remembers the helplessness of being a child. i know you remember being tiny. and i want you to know the importance of that knowledge. it is fundamental wisdom. please stop repressing it. you can be vulnerable and i won't think of you as less of a man.

you can be a real man and: express affection for your male friends, fuck guys, love eating pussy, take it up the ass, have feelings, like fashion, give a shit about stuff, feel pain, say no, cry, be wrong, learn from your mistakes, grow. you can be a real man and: tell your girlfriend you love her in public, show respect to the women in your life, not laugh at sexist and homophobic jokes, not condone sexual violence. you can be a real man and: admit that you have been victimized and need to heal, desire body types not represented in the media, not have a huge dick, not want to take part in violence.

we have to move away from these narrow, violent, misogynist, homophobic definitions of masculinity and/or manhood. this shit is toxic. we need to let little boys cry and listen to lady gaga if they want to. we need to establish a culture that raises boys to be men who respect and love themselves and who don't seek power through domination (out of a desperate fear of being dominated and humiliated). i want to tell you guys that i am committed to that culture. i'm not going to make fun of the size of your dick and i'm not going to laugh at you for having feelings and i can think of you as a whole person.

can you do the same for me?

can you unobjectify my body? can you purge yourself of the toxic messages you have learned about women's sexuality? can you handle it if i reject you? can you love me unpossesively? can you fuck me in a way that is more than a validation of your manhood? do you have to put your dick inside me every time we fuck? can we just be friends? can we have a conversation without you staring at my tits? can you take rape seriously, please? we aren't asking for it. i mean it. and i know you know it's true.

will you take the time to think about this shit? will you talk to your friends about it? are you committed to a culture where women are treated like human beings? does sexual violence offend and disgust you? if so, how are you committed to that ethic in your everyday life?

if not, what are you lying to yourself about? what have you done, condoned, looked away from that you are now afraid of facing? why does acknowledging my humanity terrify you?

we need to move past stereotypes of feminists as man-haters. hating men would be an easy solution. but life's not that easy. people, human beings, are fucking beautiful and lovable. it is not so easy to write them off. i love human beings and a lot of human beings are men and i want to be able to talk to you, have relationships with you, pass you on the street, change the world together in a way where we can both be full human beings. i am looking at you straight on, level in the eye, and i am asking you, can you recognize my humanity and your own? because i am committed to this. i want us both to be full human beings.

forgiveness and love

whoever you are, whatever you've done, there is a place for you, there is forgiveness and love. i've tried fighting hate with hate, it doesn't work, it only multiplies the problem. i have learned to feel love and forgiveness even for my perpetrators. that doesn't mean that i don't hold them accountable for their actions, i do. but i do not seek revenge and i do not wish them harm. i wish them only healing because i understand that they are sick and hurting and damaged, like i am, like we all are. i bless them. i acknowledge the truth of what they did and hold them accountable for it and i hope that they are set free. love is the essence of everything and everyone. we are made of love, we long to love and to be loved. we have been hurt, badly. we have not been taught how to love and how to be loved. we've gotten all fucked up with power and violence and pain. but i believe there is a way back, for all of us. i endeavour to work from a place of love in all that i do. i endeavour to see and value the life force of all and to devalue and damage none. i know that i am hurting and damaged and fucked up too and that i will continue to fuck up, but i am working on doing it less, i am working on centreing myself in and always starting from love. love is the question and love is the answer. and all of us are deserving. every last one.

unleash

truth is hard to carry, hard to handle. it dissolves easily into what would be easier, easier to believe. truth is ugly, it hurts my hands and back to carry it. it's messy. it spills. but i can't tell your lies anymore even as i am still telling them. there is an honesty that erupts from my body, that insists that this is not okay. i feel this way. i do. and my feelings are telling their own truth. it did happen. it is real. and all the pretending in the world just covers it over. it doesn't undo it. nothing can. i want to apologize. i feel guilty for saying the truth, for telling the police, for spilling our dirty secrets so carefully kept all over the floor in the light of day where everyone can see. i want to keep your secret but i can't anymore. it is killing me. it is eating me alive like a cancer. it is spreading and spreading and devouring me. i am not myself when i tell your lies and so i have not been myself in such a long time. and you can't face it. you are angry or you are sad. you are tired or you are still in denial. you still think everything is okay. you think it's me, that i am fucked up, messed up, that i need to heal. and i do. but my healing will only spill more truth, my healing will only bring more words to the mess. it will only shine more light on the ugliness. i am sorry and i shouldn't be. that is how well trained i am. i believe it is my responsibility to hold and hide the truth, to manipulate it and distort it until it looks like something else, something safe and presentable, something good. but it is not my responsibility and it's not possible to contain. my body will tell the truth. i will get drunk and scream and cry and throw fits. i will slice myself up with razors blades and gush blood that tells the truth.

i will act crazy. and i have done all of that and i am tired and now i can't let my body do the speaking for me, unleashing what i have worked so hard to repress. now i must be honest and let it be what it is. and it is. it is.

better for it

deep into the depths which have no end and up into the limitless skies. we are wise. i thought what i had seen, what i had known, what had been done to me, had ruined me. i mourned. i grieved. i nullified. i embraced nihilism. i lost touch. i destroyed myself. undone. undoing. i did not believe there was anything good left. i had been betrayed by all i had loved including my own self. i had done that which i swore i would never do. i had given up. i crossed the river. i thought it ruined me. i was destroyed. the endlessness of endlessness, the infinite infinity, the words which are not words, which are only sounds and which are soundless. the heart that still beats. the time that slows down or stops or rushes forward with such inconsistency. i was being reborn. it was painful. it was so painful to lose everything i loved, everything i thought i needed, everything that i believed. collapse. deep into the depths of the endlessness and soar high into the heights which defy measurement. we can go there and still live. we can be who we have been and still love. we can hurt like we hurt and still heal. there is always good to be found. i wrap my arms around the girl i was, the girl i am, i pull her close to me and hold her. i love you unconditionally. my life is worth saving. this journey has wizened me. i am a ripe fruit, a seed, the smell of decay. i am a promise broken, a new beginning, the ability to walk away. i have lived through this. lived to tell. lived to live again.

first drunk

the first time i had a drink was the first time i got hammered. i went to a get-together in brampton with a friend i didn't know well and three other people i'd never met. they were all in their early twenties. i was sixteen. i confessed that i'd never had a drink before and they all thought it was cute. they mixed vodka and a little sugar in a cup for me. i drank it. and then there was another mixed drink, some various juices and more vodka. before i knew it i had a litre of pepsi in one hand and a bottle of red wine in the other, taking fast swigs over the sink, spilling liquid down my face, getting as much into me as possible. i was drunk, i was alive, i was happy and all i wanted was more. they tried to pry the wine from my hands and in the struggle i ended up smashing it. i started crying, crying, crying. the weight of the whole world and all my pain was ripping through me. one of the guys, another girl's boyfriend, took me off into a side room to talk me down. and we talked for hours. i told him about myself. how i was two people living in one body. how my grandfather had made out with me. how all the bad things happened to violet and indigo came back when it was over. he listened to me. he was kind. suddenly he was beautiful, with his long, long mohawk, which he wore down his back. i knew i was in love with him and i had never been happier. because someone cared, someone listened, someone forgave me my insanity. he said of my freakout 'hey, it happens to all of us'. and the other guy, my friend's boyfriend, he had been asking me sexual questions that made me uncomfortable but my lips were loose and i answered, i said and it seemed i couldn't stop the words. but oh well. i was drunk and i was here and for tonight these people were my friends. and then, my friend, the girl, i confessed to her that i had crushed on her for months but that i'd never said anything, i had been too shy and scared. and she was so happy because she liked me too. and she started making out with me, but i wasn't sure that i wanted to and i couldn't say that, and she was on top of me, touching herself and i was scared. i wasn't ready for that kind of physicality. i wanted comfort. i wanted words. then her boyfriend came into the room and saw us together and he started freaking out. he freaked the fuck out and screamed at her for what seemed like hours and i tried to intervene but it only made it worse and he took off running out of the house. the night was over. and everyone passed out but i couldn't sleep. i felt alive for the first time in my life. i was strangely happy and lit up and glowing. and in the morning they walked me to the bus stop and one of the girls made a joke about split personalities and the guy who had been kind to me the night before, he gave me a knowing, sympathetic look. and i loved him.

second drunk

the second time i touched alcohol was shortly after i turned seventeen. i was living in toronto now. i had my own little apartment. my best friend and i decided that we wanted to go to this party that he had been invited to. a party with normal teenagers who would be drinking and we were nervous as hell. my mom had bought me two six packs of vodka coolers for the party and my friend and i decided to pre-drink in my apartment. that way, we reasoned, we wouldn't be nervous. a couple bottles in and we were already wasted and decided we didn't really need to go to the party after all. we could just drink here. a couple more bottles. my friend was lying on my floor, wearing my giant black poofy skirt. i was lying on my bed and the darkness started edging in all around me. i remembered that i was bitterly unhappy. that i didn't trust my friend. that i didn't trust anybody. that i wanted to die, had wanted to die for a long time but i'd never had the courage to go through with it. i thought about it. i could do it. i could do it right now and then i wouldn't have to wake up tomorrow. i found a bottle of advil in my room and i swallowed the pills in secret, one by one by one. i reached into the bottle and found that it was empty. i had taken them all. panic quickly seized me. had i done the right thing? did i really want to die? no, no i didn't. i didn't want to die. i said to my friend "can i tell you something? promise me you won't overreact?" he looked up at me, giant skirt all fanned around him, "what?" i passed him the bottle and i told him "i took all of these". he started freaking out. i started freaking out. he called poison control and i went into the bathroom and tried to make myself puke. i couldn't bring it up. i remembered that when i was in the psych ward i had often thought of drinking my shampoo, thinking it would make me puke and they would take me to the doctor's office and then i could just grab as many pills as possible and take them all. this time i wanted to puke so i wouldn't die. so i drank the shampoo. it was horrible and it burned and it did not make me puke. i started putting my fingers down my throat and managed to puke a little bit. the puke was full of burning soapy bubbles. poison control told my friend that i needed to go to the hospital. my face was tingling and i was scared. we couldn't find my glasses. i had to go without them. we took the subway and a bus, drunk, me still trying to puke up soapy vomit and screaming and crying that i don't want to die, my friend terrified. in this state the fare person at subway still asked us for our student cards when we put in student fare. my friend reasoned with him that he needed to get me to a hospital. and somehow we got there. i drank charcoal and they hooked me up with all sorts of wires monitoring my vitals. my friend saved my life.

soul starved

what was i starved of? the right to bodily autonomy. the right to say no. the right to envision and experience sexuality as sane and safe, as wild and mine. and therefore, the right to pleasure in my body, pleasure without shame. i was starved of the freedom to love my body as i saw fit, the right to decorate my body as i saw fit, the right to experiment with my body as i saw fit. i was starved because i was turned into a possession and not granted the freedom to be a living being. my body was turned into a symbol rather than the embodiment of myself. and this all took place when i was a child. i was starved of the right to set my own boundaries, starved of the right to say my own truth, starved of the right to express my own feelings and starved of the ability to know what i know, to trust my own instincts. and so, when i finally got free, i was famished, hungry, hollow, vanquished, i was so full of need and i filled up on everything. i gorged on whatever i could wrap my fingers around, that smelled or looked or seemed like what i'd been starved of. i cut my skin open with razor blades because it felt like bodily autonomy. i drank the contents of endless bottles because it tasted like freedom to be wild. i fucked with compulsion because it seemed to be pleasure without shame. i screamed and swore and started fights with people for no reason because it resembled saying no and setting boundaries. i got high every day because it smelled like the ability to run away. i stayed in abusive relationships because i thought it was safe and it was love. and as i indulged in all these counterfeit freedoms i got further and further from my truth, my self, my knowingness. i kept consuming and it only fed the hunger, it only multiplied the emptiness. somewhere deep within me my strange and wild knowing self was crying out and whispering sweetly *this is not what you are hungry for*. i couldn't hear at first because my ears were filled with the sounds of clinking glass, the sounds of feet on pavement, the sounds of the chase, the roar of my hunger. but then i was so beaten down by my endless hunting, my bottomless emptiness, my nonstop consumption that there was a pause. in that pause i heard a voice saying *none of this will feed you*. and i listened and i learned. i am hungry for music, fingers pressed into strings, dedication and practice that does not take the form of instant gratification, i am hungry for the deepness of feeling that only comes with time and a deep, deep knowing of myself, i am hungry for listening, for me to listen to myself, what i want and i what i need and to put that into reality, i am hungry for validation of my suffering and time to heal and grieve, i am hungry for boundaries, to figure out what they are and how to implement them, i am hungry for self worth and self respect, i am hungry for community, i am hungry for spirituality and a reconnection with my lost divine, for rivers and fields and open skies, i am hungry for words, hungry for art, for the expression of all that's inside, i am hungry for freedom, to say no, to say yes and to give myself permission to decide what it is that i desire. only these things will fill me and there is time.

no longer alone

if you've been down to the very bottom of your heart, where it has splintered and cracked, if you have felt the nothingness that pulses and aches wildly, i love you. if you have been violated, broken open in places you meant to keep sealed, prodded and touched by hands you did not want touching you, i respect you. if you have thrown away everything you love, chased addiction and given up on your very self, i honour you. if you are all alone, separated from the world and even from your own being, finding solace not even in the darkness of the night, i befriend you. if you are terrified that there is no way back, that all options are closed off, that after everything you've done and what's been done to you there is no longer any point, i offer you hope. if you have suffered, if you have grieved, if you have persisted, if you have given in, if you have lost faith, if you have lost your way, you are my blood, we are connected. i cannot do this alone. i cannot pull myself up from the bottom of the ocean, from the inside of the emptiness, alone. i cannot remember the love that pulses through existence, the sacredness of being, alone. i need my fellow sufferers: survivors, addicts, fuck ups, drunks, the hopeless, the betrayed, the broken, the violated, the angry, the aching, the trapped and the lost. i am with you on this path. we are here together. we are not alone.

blue moon

under a blue moon i ask the goddesses to renew me. i walk through a field at night with the virgin, mother and crone. they each have a hand on my back. they stand around me as i dig the hole on my hands and knees in which i will lay to rest what was. they are solemn and wise. they know. under a blue moon i begin again. i shake my head, i sigh, my shoulders fall, my hands let go. the truth is i don't know. i thought i had it all figured out and i don't. now all i can do is leave my heart wide open and let it fill with the overflowing love of the goddesses. they can handle it. they know the pain. they understand it. i weep into their arms and they hold me. they stroke my hair and they tell me: *creature of mine i have missed you. i am glad that you are home.*

acknowledgements

thank you to the sober community of toronto for all the love. you are life savers.

thank you to my witch sisters: lamesha, alanna (queen pigeon), sarah, jezabel, shala, katryn, medusa, nish, kathleen and casey jean. you have each been a blessing in my life. a special thank you to casey jean, my blood sister and oldest friend.

thank you to my mom, andrea, for always encouraging me to write.

thank you to carolina for helping me to find my voice again.

thank you to the goddess Herself for blessing me with this lifetime.

and thank you for reading.

Clementine Morrigan is a multidisciplinary queer feminist artist based in Toronto. She has been writing all her life and producing zines for the past ten years. She explores trauma, sexuality, and agency within her work. When not writing, she is thinking, making art, playing guitar, riding her bike, or skateboarding. You can find more of her work at www.clementinemorrigan.com.